A Strange Way To Save You And Me

A Christmas Play
For The Small Church

Eva Juliuson

CSS Publishing Company, Inc., Lima, Ohio

A STRANGE WAY TO SAVE YOU AND ME

ISBN 0-7880-1521-4

Dedicated to each young person and adult who first had a part in this play at Memorial Christian Church. You are a very important part of my life.

May your group be as blessed as we were as we worked together to share this wonderful story!

A Strange Way
To Save You And Me

Presentation

This play is presented as a reading with the actors silently acting our their parts as the narrators read from the sides of the stage. All lights should be out except for enough light for the narrators to read by and on the stage during each scene.

Children or adults or a combination may be used in this play, since no memorization is required. All energy and focus is put into the acting. When rehearsing, encourage each actor to think like their character (think how the character must be feeling). Even children can give moving and inspiring performances when they are told to think like their character. For example, tell the shepherds to imagine how surprised and scared they would be if an angel suddenly appeared before them.

The singing by the choir or congregation provides time to set up the next scene and set the mood. Background music may be played softly underneath the reading and acting.

Cast Of Characters

Narrator 1	Mary
Narrator 2	Joseph
Narrator 3	Shepherds
Narrator 4	1 Angel who announces birth
Narrator 5	Other Angels
Narrator 6	3 Wise Men
Innkeeper	Choir (or group singing)
Innkeeper's wife	
Innkeeper's son	

Song: "Oh, Come, All Ye Faithful" (choir)

Narrator 1:

We're going to tell you a familiar story which has been told every year since it first happened. It's not the usual "Once upon a time" fairy tale. It's part of the most truthful story ever told. You've probably heard it before, and most likely you'll hear it again. But today, listen with new ears and an open heart. This story never grows old and never ends!

Narrator 2:

There once was a time when Caesar Augustus, who was a Roman emperor, announced a census should be taken. He ordered a counting of all the people so they could be taxed. Everyone was required to go to the hometown of his ancestors to be officially registered. Since Joseph was a descendent of King David, he had to go to the city of Bethlehem. It was a long and difficult journey, for Joesph's young wife traveled with him, even though she was due to have a baby any time. The roads were rocky and dusty as the donkey carried Mary towards Bethlehem. Joseph hoped they could make it to shelter before it was Mary's time to give birth.

Song: "Oh Little Town Of Bethlehem" (choir)

Narrator 2:

Now the city of Bethlehem was filled with noise and people who had come from everywhere to register for the census. Some were grumbling about having to leave their homes and come to Bethlehem just so the Romans could tax them even more heavily. Others were filled with excitement, for they seldom got to come to the big city. Then there were the businesspeople in Bethlehem who were thrilled with the extra business the census brought them.

(Innkeeper's wife enters holding a bowl and stirring with a wooden spoon. The lights go on the stage.)

All the inns around town had quickly filled up. There were no rooms left anywhere. At one such inn, the innkeeper's wife was busy trying to cook enough extra food for all their customers.

(Innkeeper rushes in.)

Her husband came running in to report he had just rented out their own room to another family. There were already people sleeping everywhere on the floor. Just as well, shrugged the wife. They probably wouldn't be getting much sleep anyway with all these people to clean and cook for.

(Innkeeper's son enters.)

Just then, their young son, who also served as their stable boy, ran in, saying, "Father, Father, there's a young couple at the door. They need somewhere to stay tonight!"

The innkeeper grumbled, "Can't you see we have no room left? Tell them to go somewhere else."

"But, Father," pleaded the young boy, "his wife is about to have a baby any time now!"

"That's not my problem!" announced the innkeeper.

The innkeeper's wife seldom disagreed with her husband, but this was different. "It just wouldn't be right for a baby to be born out on the street! We must do something!"

"I know!" said the little stable boy. "They can stay in the stable out back! It's warm and safe and the straw makes a good bed."

"It's better than nothing," said the wife. "Son, go show them the way and let them know that if they need anything, I'll try to help."

The innkeeper shrugged in resignation as the young boy ran to take Joseph and Mary out to the stable.

(Everyone leaves stage.)

Song: "Away In A Manger" (solo)

(As Narrator 3 reads, the stable boy leads Joseph and Mary back on stage to a stall with an empty manger and a bale of hay for Mary to sit on.)

Narrator 3:

The boy led Mary and Joseph to the stable. The animals made low sounds as they curiously observed these new arrivals in their domain. There was still one vacant stall. The boy showed them to it and spread out some clean hay for them.

Joseph gently helped Mary sit down on the makeshift bed. Mary was in a lot of discomfort by this time from the trip and from the beginning of labor. She tried to hide her pain from her husband, for she could see his concern for her.

The young boy asked if they needed a blanket. Joseph told him they had brought some from home and began to unpack what they would need.

The little stable boy shyly said, "I have a really good blanket I will bring for your baby. It's not new. In fact, my mother made it for me when I was a baby. I'll go get it. I'm getting too old for it now. It will be good for your baby. Is there anything else you need?"

"No, thank you, my little friend," smiled Joseph as he tousled his hair. "You have been very helpful."

The young boy left and Joseph turned his attention back to Mary. *(Stable boy exits.)* He was worried, for neither of them knew much about having a baby. They were far from home and all the women who usually helped with such things.

Mary saw his anxious expression and smiled reassuringly, "Don't worry, for the Lord is with us."

This was just an ordinary night — yet it was a night like no other!

(Mary and Joseph exit.)

Song: "Sweet Little Jesus Boy" (solo)

(As Narrator 4 reads, shepherds enter and rest while watching sheep. Some could be standing, leaning on their staffs, while others could be sitting or sleeping.)

Narrator 4:

That same night, there were shepherds who were guarding their sheep in the fields outside of Bethlehem. It was an unusually clear night with the stars shining brighter than ever. The shepherds were glad to be in the still, peaceful countryside, instead of in the noisy city. They had seen travelers going past them on the road toward the city all week. City people often made fun of the shepherds, for they were dirty and smelled like sheep. Out in the fields under the stars, they could be themselves.

(The first angel appears onstage.)

As they rested, suddenly an angel appeared before them. The glory of the Lord was so bright, it frightened them. The angel said, "Do not be afraid! I'm here to bring you the most joyful news ever announced, and it's for everyone! The Savior — yes, the Messiah, the Lord — was born tonight in Bethlehem. You will know it is him, for he will be wrapped in swaddling clothes and lying in a manger."

(Rest of the angels appear from offstage behind the first.)

Then a whole host of angels appeared, all singing praises to God for sending peace and goodwill to men.

Song: "Angels We Have Heard On High" (choir)

(Angels exit stage as narrator begins again.)

Narrator 4:
When the angels disappeared into heaven again, the shepherds rejoiced at what they had seen and heard. They could scarcely believe that God cared enough for them that he sent his angels to tell them of the Messiah's birth!

"Let's go to Bethlehem and see for ourselves this wonderful thing the Lord has made known to us!"

(Shepherds hurriedly exit.)

They ran to Bethlehem, somehow knowing their lives would never be the same again. This time Bethlehem didn't seem cruel or menacing, for they knew the hope of all the world was born in Bethlehem.

Song: "Away In A Manger" (Children or choir)

(Joseph and Mary sitting in stable on stage. Mary could be cuddling and rocking the baby.)

Narrator 5:

In the stable, Joseph and Mary cuddled their newborn baby and marveled at their tiny miracle, as all new parents do. Joseph was so relieved that all had gone well with his sweet wife and this tiny little boy the Lord had entrusted to him. There was still so much that he didn't understand about this special baby. After all, God had made known to him that this was to be the Messiah, the Savior. Right now, he was like any other helpless little baby who was depending on Joseph to care and provide for him. Joseph felt a great responsibility to love and protect his wife and new son.

(Shepherds and stable boy get ready to enter.)

A group of men in rough clothing entered the stable. Joseph's first instinct was to shield Mary and the baby, so he stepped in front. Then he noticed the little stable boy had brought them, so he relaxed a little.

"Who are you? What do you want?" asked Joseph.

"We are shepherds from the fields just outside of town. We don't wish to disturb you, but we have come to see for ourselves the baby which is Christ, the Lord."

Joseph was surprised at what they said and asked them, "Who told you this news? Our baby's name is Jesus."

So great was their excitement that all the shepherds began speaking at once. Then one of the shepherds spoke for the whole group, telling Mary and Joseph all the things the angel had told them. He recounted how the angel had told them they would find the baby lying in a manger, and here he was! The shepherds told them of the awesome choir of angels which had come from heaven, praising God for this wonderful thing!

Reluctantly, the shepherds told Joseph and Mary they would leave so the mother and baby could get some rest. Before they left, they bowed in humble adoration before their Lord. They said they would tell all their families and friends about this wonderful thing which had happened. They said, "Praise God, for we have seen the Lord when he first came to earth!"

They bowed and quietly left to go back to their sheep.

(All the shepherds leave the stage.)

Joseph and Mary looked at one another, somehow knowing their little Jesus would never truly belong to them alone, for he was for all people. They solemnly wondered what this meant for their little family.

(Joseph and Mary stay on stage during song, cuddling baby.)

Song: "A Strange Way To Save The World"* (solo)

Narrator 6:
Later on, there were other visitors: three richly dressed men who were led by the little stable boy.

The young boy explained that these wise men came from far away. They had come to the inn looking for the child who would be king some day. They had followed a star which led them to this place.

"It seemed very important, so I brought them to you," said the little boy.

Joseph said, "Please come into this humble place."

Mary and Joseph looked on in amazement as the three rich men came forward and knelt in worship and adoration of their little baby.

The first wise men set a gift of gold by the wooden manger and said, "May his life be a rich blessing to all people."

The second visitor moved closer to the child and offered a gift of frankincense, a strong and fragrant spice from the East.

"I bring myrrh," said the third man. "It is bitter, for this baby's life will not be easy. He will have bitterness and pain, but others will receive strength from him."

They quietly and reverently worshiped little baby Jesus. As they were leaving, they said, "May others be led to him as we were. May God bless you and the child."

They left to go back to their homes, yet they would never be the same again, for they had come to know their Savior and King!

(Joseph and Mary stay on stage.)

Narrator 1:
This is the story of how Jesus first came into the world, but it doesn't end here. It's really just the beginning. It's more than history, for that little baby who was born so long ago still lives! He is born anew in each of us when we bow in humble adoration just as the shepherds and wise men did. Our lives will never be the same. We become new creatures. We are given new life, for he is our Emmanuel, which means "God is with us!"

Think about it! The awesome, powerful Creator of all the universe doesn't just sit on his throne in heaven and look down on us. He loves us! He loves us so much that he sent us all his love wrapped in the tiny form of a fragile newborn baby who came to serve us and be with us!

He didn't come as one would expect a king to come. He didn't come as one would expect the son of God to come. He was born in the most simple, humble, ordinary surroundings. He still comes that way today. He comes into our lives when we acknowledge him as our king. Then he transforms our ordinary lives into something very holy. As we make him total King of our lives, we help bring his kingdom here on earth. What joy there is in helping his Kingdom grow in ordinary everyday life! What a strange way for God to save the world! What a strange way to save you and me!

Song: "Joy To The World!" *(Everyone sings.)*

*Sound track available from Benson Music Group, Inc. (615-742-6800). Choral arrangement also available, composed by Allen, Mauldin, Clark, Cope, and Harris.

12